BEAUTIFUL

ZERO

BEAUTIFUL ZERO

POEMS

JENNIFER WILLOUGHBY

MILKWEED EDITIONS

Published 2015 by Milkweed Editions
Printed in Canada
Cover design by Mary Austin Speaker
Cover photo/illustration by Mary Austin Speaker
Author photo by Kurt Gegenhuber
15 16 17 18 19   5 4 3 2 1
First Edition

Milkweed Editions, an independent nonprofit publisher, gratefully acknowledges sustaining support from the Jerome Foundation; the Lindquist & Vennum Foundation; the McKnight Foundation; the National Endowment for the Arts; the Target Foundation; and other generous contributions from foundations, corporations, and individuals. Also, this activity is made possible by the voters of Minnesota through a Minnesota State Arts Board Operating Support grant, thanks to a legislative appropriation from the arts and cultural heritage fund, and a grant from the Wells Fargo Foundation Minnesota. For a full listing of Milkweed Editions supporters, please visit www.milkweed.org.

Library of Congress Cataloging-in-Publication Data

Willoughby, Jennifer, 1970-
[Poems. Selections]
Beautiful zero : poems / Jennifer Willoughby.
pages cm
ISBN 978-1-57131-480-2 (paperback) -- ISBN 978-1-57131-942-5 (ebook)
I. Title.
PS3623.I57765A6 2016
811'.6--dc23

2015022371

Milkweed Editions is committed to ecological stewardship. We strive to align our book production practices with this principle, and to reduce the impact of our operations in the environment. We are a member of the Green Press Initiative, a nonprofit coalition of publishers, manufacturers, and authors working to protect the world's endangered forests and conserve natural resources. *Beautiful Zero* was printed on acid-free 100% postconsumer-waste paper by Friesens Corporation.

For Kurt Robert Gegenhuber

CONTENTS

COME CLOSE THEN BACK AWAY

Time: sunset. I am having a clearly defined feeling.
You are lost in immaculate self-regard.
Those diaphanous spores are copulating.
You are giving me disco lessons.
Dance fast and lead with your ass.
Without fear, my body would come apart.
Look at me go.
Just because you know me doesn't mean I am real.
My kneesocks nestle at my feet.
Then we create an adult situation.
You do what you did yesterday.
It was great.
A record player is skipping in the distance.
You hit it with your fist.
I'm drowning myself again.
It's my new tradition.
The power of obsession lies.
It drives me but I can't arrive.
Time: sunrise. I have to wear glasses.
I have to imagine a small crowd of people who need me.
It's hard to make friends with a column of oxygen.
You try.
Everyone tries.
The trees treat me like fire.

THE PROPERTIES OF WOMEN
ARE THE PROPERTIES OF LIFE

Do we attract iron filings? Yes, each follicle
buzzes with steel. Do we penetrate healthy tissue?
Yes, our amazing fingers leave self-sealing scars.
Do we ingest chemicals? Yes, we wrestle our feelings
into flammable capes. Do we enter and leave our feelings?
Yes, we wear young antlers to confuse hunters. Do we
represent disaster? Yes, it smells like sulfur after we rain.
Do we lack an organizing principle? Yes, we do not follow
a traditional axis. Do we howl and snap? Yes, it's the only
way to communicate with our demographic. Do we circle
the house like any stray predator? Yes, and our teeth shine on.

DO NOT BE BROKEN BY THE DAY

Take it from me, Caroline, a crisis of faith
is not as interesting as a dead pigeon
in the cistern after a long winter.
The world doesn't want to see you
on your knees for more than a minute
when it could be inspecting a music
box that knew how to fly.
Your gorgeous *cabeza* is cold
as a gun's empty chamber, a hole
that can't be stuffed with poems or
the half-chewed aspirin of the moon.
Feral and barrel-chested, a pigeon knows
why bacteria can't sleep at night and hears
the trees catch three incurable diseases.
We can be a vessel. My sad Caroline,
if we get Emerson's idea that observing
the physical exfoliates the spiritual, then
isn't forensic investigation where it's at?
A bird is an object that breaks light
into patterns so we can come out
of our houses to say goodbye to the trees.

THE WHOLE UGLY EMPIRE

For a while it was nothing but
Goodbye, Ruby Tuesday and jugs
of Gallo in wood-paneled basements. We
lived in the blaze of shame and statement,
in the battlefield of family, choked with slow-
growing rhizomes and leviathan desire.
Shy, shy, chubby, and inviolate—
we husked Polaroid film to freeze
Paris and Amarillo clouds so that our darkness
was not always a wall. We got our hopes up.
We folded our clothes and went somewhere
international and dank. Time seals all wounds.
We got over it. We looked at history and history
looked bright: chandelier antlers in the Sheraton
ballroom, Jackie O's glittering sheath. Years
from now we're still riding it out in the night where
the rain makes it look like we've lived here all our lives.

BE NOT INHOSPITABLE TO STRANGERS

By now smitten by fish and fluid
dynamics, I join the boat's vernal
operations to map our arctic spheres
like a pirate x's gold in paradise.
I am in love with sojourn. I am
in love with things loosened
and relinquished, as a tooth.
The contents of the vials
are as follows: vintage cyanide,
baby doll eyes, and music to help
me stop smoking. I know a little
science and it will take the children
of a glacial basin to fix the failings
of a fallen world. Blake says the bat
has left the brain that won't believe
but I think every thing wants out
of a man-made cage. My platoon
surges with overcast hope. Penguins
plunge over the double hull driven by
mackerel and glands and the ghosts
of wives who don't scientifically exist.
To the left: ice long gone. To the right:
something small gone crazy. Above us: no
Christ. Below us: the television stays off all night.

FUN HOUSE

Tonight I am getting smaller,
without chanting, my mouth
is gone like the moon wiped
off the horizon. I have one
arm. I have three heads. The
house clicks on its electronic
eye. My spine compacts like
a cat. My hair smears dirt off
my body. I fight myself sideways.
The house cordons me off.
An instinct splinters. The house
is looking for something left
behind. A scent. A snowy molar.
A reflection can be a manhunt.
Describe the last time you saw
her. Describe her erratic behavior.
Do you know how much a mirror
conceals. A thump. A crack. A sound
of unlatching. I am getting taller.
The rubber ache of organs stretched.
My brain shines like a lung. My hair
reaches out to the trees. I can see 360
degrees. A feeling of correct perspective.
Wispy membranes where I was going
to be. I bring you the terrible pieces.

THE ONE YOU HAVE TO LOVE

I'm being raised in
a documentary about
difficult children. One
of us hums. A poster
of the solar system
goes up in flames.
The trees don't know if
this will ever get better.
Normal is a monogram
you wear when everyone
stares. The cameraman
is placid and tan. I am
blurry. I am not in this
shot. There I am, wearing
my velveteen ears. Life is
my new enemy but life
vibrates. Sometimes you
can't take your hands off it.

SHARK WEEK

They say okay, nature, we are here to participate.
They are creating my costume—tofu smooth,
iceberg blue. They say go Brando. Motivation:
Hunger beyond reason. Need without doubt.
No question, method is best. Surf's up. Main
cues: Mackerel and sadness. They say more wow.
Machine guns. Maybe I have trouble at home.
Subplot: Hunt seals is the job for the day.
They say no emotion. Give us blood and sunshine.
Teamsters won't chum, budget troubles. I say
so what. Chum is dumb. Law of jungle: Some hunger
makes no sound. Gaffer goes splash. Adios, gaffer!
They say "perfect killing machine." I say no shame.
The ocean loves me and the ocean is totally normal.

THEIR JOY IS RIGHT IN FRONT OF THEM

Today the babies are everywhere I am,
underfoot, but in a good way like sunshine.
One baby loves bluster and migrates west.
Just because that baby is angry does not
mean he's a fascist. That baby likes anything
pineapple. One baby loves to hunker down
in the yard, her mission is related to chickens.
That baby's named Chad, he is not very popular.
One baby hovers above my head, attempting to
illustrate the physics of astral projection. It finally
clicks, how I can just drop my neural load and go.
That baby is invisible. That baby was a baby in
another life, too, only her mothers were wolves.
That baby invents auroral light with a few ice cubes.
One baby shares my adorable mood disorder. That
baby knows once I wasn't in my right mind. Um, hi
baby, I'm keeping my eye on you. That baby sleeps
in a fat blue house and she is something beautiful.

BRINGING IN THE NOIR

Here comes the vile season
and we are always checking the sky
for falling pilots and the green nimbus
that indicates disaster. A hint of disaster
acts like catnip on the hippocampus
and we are galloping through the yard
in striped pajamas and checking the sky
for government drones and we are speaking
the language of love to our animals. And frat
boys jellyfish our alley on their way to oblivion,
all high fives and pants-around-the-ankles while
we get physical over toast and a serious game
of Candyland. A whiff of competition blasts
our synapses and we go all William Golding
on the ass of the night and we kill the lights
and interrupt the movie. And the movie is about
betrayal and the California landgrab. A memory
rusts out the heroine's mouth while we check
the roof for damage. Roman Polanski unzips
our repressed memories with geography. There's
the Owens Valley aqueduct! There's the Biltmore
façade! And we eat corn muffins and ravish our
verdant home. And we glide through the buffalo
dust while the nation goes Soviet on human
relations. And we speak our cruddy little language
of love and recall how in those days, the girls
became witches and pilots and business executives.
And we all write our own folksongs to carry the hurt
like a purse filled with ingenious and frivolous things.

HOW WE LOVE GEOGRAPHY

O my incumbent Americans, my giant pioneers,
my over-confident drivers, it's not like this place
was ever really respectable. Not a place to go
for Mother's Day or to fritter away a humid
June evening. Here it's a matter of record
that if a man goes undercover as a hobo to see
the real world his heart will be broken by ham
and eggs and then mended by Veronica Lake,
but if a man turns into a werewolf during
the full moon his own father will shoot him.
There's not much room for sunflowers but
if you drop a little acid you can see the true
beauty of Cielo Drive before Manson carved
his star-shaped holes in California. Go north
where winter hits the plains like roller skates
tossed off a freeway overpass and you can see
the world's largest ball of twine made by one man.
In St. Rose, Louisiana you can see the world's
largest pecan tree, Zachary Taylor's bathtub
and the back-roads grave of Hitler's horse.
Today all the pilots thank god for NASA
and land our best swift passengers.

RANGER BUSTER JANGLE

Make way for Jesus or what have you
and now we are all sons-of-bitches, says
Professor Bainbridge in the desert
when the sterilized light cracks open
like a twenty-kiloton skull and I'm
never in the sixth grade again.
Breakfast floods the flame-retardant
neighborhoods, studded with plastic
juice cups from Yuma, Kickapoo
and Quince. We go crazy for citrus
and Victory Gin but we smell totally
liturgical—amber, blasted cedar, ash.
The next decade bellies up to the bar
and my hair looks like the death of
romance. At night I sit still as an American
wife, thinking of the worst thing that
can happen. My hands crack and twitch.
A skywriter writes: MARIA, I LOVE YOU
into the blue. The white drifts away like
a swan. In the biosphere of my eye, a cloud.

ST. DECEIVER IN THE GARDEN

As the women, we are sometimes
left to our own devices like sucking
up lint or writing haiku for famous
people until the bells call us back to
the circle of light. I don't know what
movie we're starring in today, the one
with fur-cloaked madman on campus
or the romantic comedy where the heroine
lives in a tree. The costumes are to die for—
chartreuse balloons with slits that split
to reveal an ancient version of our worst
hangover. We bang our erstwhile sexiness
like airport tambourines while craft services
ties two thousand starlings to the rafters:
they are playing the part of Nature and can
bathe in Perrier if they want. Periodically
we take a break for raw carrots and chat
about past incarnations as Dancer at Xanadu
and Nurse on the Hospital Roof. The makeup
artist fixes our floribunda scars and says:
it doesn't matter how much money you make,
the man you get is the man you hate.

WE SEEK A SHEPHERD OR A SIGN

The religion of spring is simple.
How to fix the wicker, where to
spread the birdseed. A wedding
we attend features a never-ending
blessing. Friends assemble. Friends depart.
There is the blessing of the big white dress
and the unbuttoned tux. The blessing of fish
and the last snatched minute of lust under
the coats. Finished by gin and frosting,
we pass out cigarettes and hooray our
way home. You tell me in the fever
dreams of money everything burns.
I tell you the neighbors are saving
up for a baby. There is nothing special
about renting. Your neck is wide open.
You whisper stories into my lap.
A little blackbird goes to the moon,
seeking a way to sleep through dawn.
I say come on. I say yeah, right. Rain
springs me another leak in the ceiling.
Your brushstroke grows uneven. I'm
waiting for the devil to make me an offer.
Oh, hatchet man. Oh, chatterbox. Reach
me, reluctant, under the coats. Sometimes
what gathers doesn't move.

LOSING THE PLOT

If this were a movie we'd be in love
already or planning the overthrow
of Florida. But I am not an ingénue
and you never learned to float. I
wish I was a famous writer high
on ketamine and Clairol but what
I remember is summers selling waxy
lipstick door-to-door. If this were a movie
you'd be dressed as Groucho Marx,
happily patting my ass, saying *you're only
as young as the woman you feel*. We'd stroll
the avenue, swinging our arms like children.
When we die, we both want to be buried
on top of Marilyn Monroe. If this were
a quiz show, we'd be winning big with
our novelty tricks. You, always knowing
which astronaut played golf on the moon
and me, not resembling anyone's mother.

THESE BONES WILL RISE AGAIN

They say the age of irony is dead
so I put on my glasses and prepare
to be a vehicle of complete sincerity.
Say cheese, America! I love you as
a Christian loved the catacombs,
a place of both advancement
and retreat. The dollar falls so I
go to church in search of something
that will last forever. There are faces
desolated by their children, their lack
of children, their age and occupation.
There are faces made whole by a faith
not everyone can name. I take the hand of
a holy man, what he don't know won't
hurt him. Then I gather with the knitters,
thinking how Dickens would love us, our
fragrant wrists that contain a rage no man
can cure. Oh Mathilda. Oh Christine. Come
back here, America! I will share two secrets.
I am afraid to been seen while exercising. I
am not afraid of corpses. I trust you, America!
Your pilgrim hands take no getting used to
and my help comes from the mailbox where
all our days of reckoning are born.

COUNTRY ON FIRE

You're not the only one who does weird
stuff down in Florida where the fear of the current
economy makes you stockpile atomic testing
helmets and question studious men who
measure the intensity of connections from
beyond the grave. I stand next to a Key West
crypt whose inscription reads: *I told you I was sick.*
In the lemony heat, love brings love to whomever
refuses to fall to her knees. In one scenario, we
go down with the plane. In another, we are saved
by a godlike cloud. You are gentle. I have
a skeleton. We don't think any president can
save us. Living in this country is like finding
the weapon that solves the crime. No one claps,
but the wait is over. Blaze on, Florida, blaze on.

MEMOIR SO FAR

I am born. I am a merry-go-round of sound.
Brass-tasseled evergreens surround my house.
The trend is embellishment—beaded wings,
printed skins and wire-thin lariats of gold.
I half-manage fractions, atoms and Lady
Macbeth. Beautiful is not for me. Suddenly,
I am a sculpture. Visitors come from far away
to inspect my edges. Danger does not make me
valuable. I am the state of California without
opening my eyes. The state of California is
the color of flying. Now a goddamn slash slits
my ribs and out pops a rabbit. This trick
takes practice. Mine is the wonder. Mine
is the thunder. Mine is the body of gold.
When am I born? Not in a thousand years.

BLUNDER

Too bad you don't have
zodiac moments, seeing
patterns of disaster before
they happen. I live in
the current conditions.
Aging is a current condition.
The house is solidly in the now.
Familiar the need for estrangement.
Impossible without the past.
Just the other day, I looked
away for a minute. You came
back wearing a white lab coat,
ready to amputate. I lack the rigor
of the early recordings. There is
still raw artistry when I sleep.
Sometimes a casual obsession
is the worst. I taught myself
to smoke in summer. Naked,
I needed to feel the heat.

THIS YEAR HAS MY NAME ON IT

Then it is January and it's the year
of the horse but I don't love the idea
of an animal standing in for the passage
of time. Animals are magic and time
pops with dumb quotidian stuff: Year
of our first kiss. Year of crumbling ducts.
Year another sequin had to be removed
from the solar system. Notice how I violate
your sense of personal space the second
I open my eyes. If January is two trains
traveling in opposite directions, I am not
on either train. Maybe if I go away, I'll
embrace what it means to be here. How I
am lonely. How I am surrounded by animals.
How I must lift my eyes to the greenless trees,
snow-humped gutters and seizing machinery.
I need an object to light my face like a love
scene. First comes the high-gloss belly
of a jet. Then the moon's beautiful zero.
Here it comes. Here it comes again.

KAISER VARIATIONS 1

You've had ten years to tell me everything
you know about the Atchafalaya Swamp,
the mangled devastation of its buffer marshes,
the spectacular ascension of egrets and two-
winged anhinga. Remember sliding shirtless
into the hospital bed while I was circling
the drain at Kaiser Permanente? The man
on TV driving the convertible in a gorilla suit
was Robert Wagner, his middling skills
nobilized by the death of Natalie Wood,
she of the alabaster hands and green bikini.
Love cannot be our tragedy. Recall how, while
cracking my cast like an icicle, the night surgeon
said: The more you love, the more you turn into
an object, a beloved horse standing in the rain.

KAISER VARIATIONS 2

I was bleeding profusely at Kaiser Permanente,
sky-high on morphine like the sad vampire
in *Bela Lugosi Meets A Brooklyn Gorilla.*
Why must age and degradation always stick
together like fungus on a rock? Thank god
you came along to braid my hair and play
checkers, just like old times, before the polar
bears were dying and we all got poor without
even trying. On clean hospital sheets, we re-
enacted July 20, 1969, where I was the moon
and you were the lunar module. The night
surgeon arrived with my missing digit in a soup
bowl and said: Kids, we may not be able to see
the stars from this window, but they're there.

KAISER VARIATIONS 3

It was the fourth quarter of the Badger-Buckeye
game and I smashed the neutrality rule eleven
times in the psych ward at Kaiser Permanente.
The QB landed a hook and ladder pass, I dissolved
a little Librium under my tongue and the night
counselor talked about emotions. Big or small,
emotions were cocaine and I craved a billion while
poor Vivian got defeated by a group hug.
Counselor said: The speaking is easy but the feeling
is hard. I was stuck in throes of accuracy, unplugging
my childhood of unimproved love. Man down!
Man down on the field, Bucky oompa'd a cute
tuba player, one more field goal to go and the kicker's
toe rose like a flag, true north and beautiful. Night counselor
said: It's a gift from god, motherfucker, no two ways about it.

KAISER VARIATIONS 4

I was having my heart started with sizzling
paddles in the pale sinister halls of Kaiser
Permanente and I was feeling revived as an old
steel mill on the first day of a brand new war.
Then you blew in with pictures of Indianapolis
and your Meyer Lansky trench coat and what
could we do but snuggle? There is something
about a hospital that makes it easy to redefine
desire as the absence of wires. The night
surgeon tied up my loose ends and said: It
would have been fun to be in Havana while
Eartha Kitt sang "When Smoke Gets In Your
Eyes" to a roomful of New Jersey gangsters
but even romance can be ugly and survive.

KAISER VARIATIONS 5

I was riding high on my slim artificial limb
courtesy of the good people at Kaiser Permanente.
The way the prophets tell it, I had nowhere
to go but up although it's just as easy to go down
with a hinge in your fibula. While I was forbidden
to operate heavy machinery we found fresh
ways to tingle. We drank the apple juice
provided and banned conversations ending
in why. The remaining bones grew fidgety
and shy, wary of the stranger in their lives.
The night surgeon arrived with extra-long socks
and said: Sure, getting old is a process of getting
burned but there are always fresh words to find the hurt.

KAISER VARIATIONS 6

One night after you told me anything
that moves is headed for destruction, I
ruptured a muscle trying to imitate a brain
in action. Propped on orthopedic boxes
in the terrycloth warmth of Kaiser Permanente,
distance was collapsing between me and the lives
of people I had never been. When I was my
mother, I smoked Kools by the community pool,
trying to remember the music that summoned
the monster. You smuggled in salami on rye
just as the night surgeon arrived with my file.
He said: Lady, a treasure hunt will soon begin.
Then you will see something interesting.

KAISER VARIATIONS 7

I was hard at work on the next generation
of parks that featured naturalistic plantings
in the ruins of grain silos along the spastic
Mississippi when I was struck by lightning.
Airlifted to the vestibular therapy ward of
Kaiser Permanente, I twisted like fiddleheads
in the wind. You brought me the book of Rilke,
his inner ear so finely tuned to insular human
music trying to get out. For old time's sake,
the surgeon arrived with a pack of Lamictal
and a small chalkboard that said (in the words
of the Norse god Thor): *When the thunder roars, go indoors.*

KAISER VARIATIONS 8

I was at the stadium protesting our deep national
sadness, cheering improved human relations
and solar power when I was knocked cold by
a pop fly and revived with ammonium nitrate
behind the olive curtain at Kaiser Permanente.
You saw the razor in all this rising and falling,
my womanly loneliness caramelized in blood.
No crybaby, no waiting for fastidious grief. I made
a vow to give up my Chekhovian sense of loss
and you promised to build me a miniature beach
complete with pelicans and pirate's gold. The night
surgeon measured the lump on my head with calipers,
decrying geometry and past-times for the masses.
Running in circles is not how to start a revolution,
he said. That's just how to hit a girl in glasses.

KAISER VARIATIONS 9

I was being revascularized in the aluminum
canals of Kaiser Permanente and it was just
what I imagine cannibalism would feel like.
John Prine says that blood looks like shadows
in a black and white video but I say it looks like
blood. Make me a vessel, lord, not a sieve.
From out of the long hallway of our marriage
you appeared as Lancelot with a comic book
and a fifth of gin. You ripped open the gray
industrial drapes to let the erotic sunshine
prick my skin, all lemon gone metallic, my
superhero cape clipped for good. The night
surgeon arrived with a vial of me. He said:
Did you know that human blood contains
albumin? We can paint a Sistine masterpiece
or simply cook it like an egg.

KAISER VARIATIONS 10

I've spent a lifetime avoiding Tolstoy's
heroine, exalted first then broken by a
moment of happiness. Marriage is waxed
with accident, contingency, and birds that
seem to mean more than what they are.
I had just lost my hand building a makeshift
village for ideological people; you opened
your arms like a wound. Easily triaged at
Kaiser Permanente, from my room we could
hear patients cheering the new president's
motorcade on its way to the beach. The night
surgeon placed a takeout order for some kung
pao shrimp and another prosthetic. Hey kids,
he said, you want to see some magic? There's
nothing we can't replace with something else.

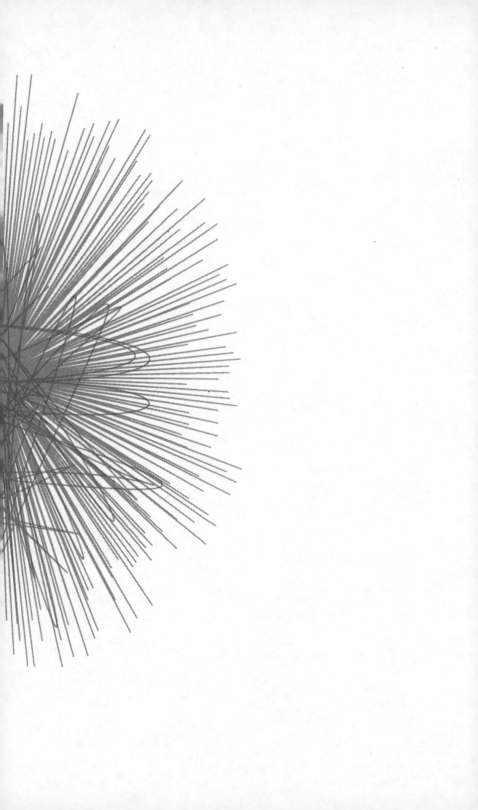

HOUSE OF SLEEP

The bed illuminates as it turns.
The bed sings in a minor key.
I love to be unconscious, again
and again and again. Now I
am wearing my powder-blue
parka of childhood and you're
wearing the mustache of my
dreams. The ladies' magazines
say not to eliminate strangeness
from a relationship. Thanks, ladies!
Love will not, love will not casually
merge into the crowd like a stalker.
A stalker has feelings deliberate as lions.
You never see a lion just making it up
as he goes along. We have been lions.
We dropped skins wherever felt right.
The stars pulsed our jungle with light.
What's great about the jungle is there
are all these ways to love you.

YOUR PROBLEM IS FOREST FIRES

Smoke. No. Ranger Bob scans the tree line.
All green. All serene. Scan, Bob, scan. His
shirt is green as nature. Bob says nature is
a dream house everyone can afford. I know
nature is a knife you don't see coming. I guess
the magic went. Used to be all trees turned
me on. Spruce, juniper, spruce. Copper beech.
Crisp whiff. White birch. Split trunks leaked
resin stink. The best incense. Start to think.
Light match: *swick*. Flame to leaf: *hiss*. Another
field trip. Kids all sticky. Ick. Think what can
burn. Hotter than inside skin. Bob says just
teach, never scare. Newsflash: Am bear. The kids
don't even care. What comes back from ashes.

WAVE IF YOU SEE ME

Glassy-eyed shadow of love, I wait
like a handkerchief in the graveyard,
to be of use. But my evenings develop
a yellow rash of paralysis and snoring.
Oi, this coffee tastes awful, I say, channeling
Eliza Doolittle, small mouth soured and no hat.
In bars, in kitchens and cars and everywhere
that time passes with a brisk slap of shame
I say, *He that has an ear, let him hear.* Meanwhile,
the nicotine gum, jumping jacks and clean
shirts—my steps to better myself—
are just rusty cudgels in your cornfield.
When the TV news covers lubrication
and the topic of death, I remember
the Palomar banana slugs that mate on
dangling ropes of slime for twenty-four
hours at a time. Most girls these days,
have you noticed, are so happy, they knit
and visit with Jesus like it was no big deal.
I pass fat bulldogs, wet lilacs, and swaggering
billboards of freedom and I think to be living
means to be seen. On that note, ikebana
lady, you should know there is no way to arrange
me. I am all short stems and thorns.

I HAVE A SECRET ADMIRER

Both of us are breathing.
One of us carries the gene
for September, maudlin
and orange. One of us makes
a bargain with god, one of us
removes an article of clothing.
One of us acts like an animal
escaping its cage in the night
to watch all of you sleep. Now
that we know how to amberize
each tiny minute of living,
the fun is gone. The first time
we meet, we trigger a dormant
hormone that consumes rational
gratification. Bang bang is how we
fight off love's frequent impossibilities.
Do not get attached to the inability
to comprehend options. On the green
phone, a dial tone. No wait, it's ringing.

THE SUN IS STILL A PART OF ME

More than ever shy is why I
am inside with the sun as my
more popular roommate.
The sun illuminates my uniform
of silence. The sun knows how
love is just the distance between
unlovable objects. My phone is lying
over there. My phone is close
to solving the mystery of why
I don't answer the phone.
I am so busy. I am practicing
my new hobby of watching me
become someone else. There is
so much violence in reconstruction.
Each minute is grisly, but I have
to participate. I am building
what I cannot break.

IT IS NOT ENTIRELY MY FAULT

We are at the wedding of your brother
and the Brooklyn princess and the apparent
failure of the polka to restore balance to
the universe wipes teenage lovers off my
list of disappointments. Oh, hello! I have
noticed you before, I think I met you
somewhere, without clothes on. You
put your mouth everywhere. Now they
are. More kissing, more clinking, when
will there be a crackdown on this sort of thing.
One martini absorbs the details, a lantern.
One hand of your hands holds my hand
through which it might absorb all the secrets
of my life, or not. I do not read leaves;
I do not have visions. What's wrong is
the difference between the declarations
of love and the love itself. There is
nothing less original than a sentence.

WISCONSIN SPACE ODYSSEY

Delayed and swirling around inside
the Dane Co. International Airport
we are counting the ways the Badger
State has made us stronger. Maybe not
with the old-time pioneers' gung-ho
approach to cross-country travel but
with the jowly tenacity of America's
Dairyland. The sky turns the color
of morning glories just before they
die and on the runway, planes
relax like ladies at a day spa. We
give up on getting somewhere
and settle for 2-man charades
and tall cans of Milwaukee beer.
You give me the first word and it
is the word for life that sounds like
falling and looks like crows in a row
on a telephone wire. A family from
Manitowoc and their cats spill down
the concourse, just like modern-day
Steinbeck and you give me the second
word. It is the word for house that smells
like apricots and tastes like a cigarette
shared at the height of imperfect passion.
Newly recruited soldiers collect free Cokes
from a stewardess and the war effort
tumbles effortlessly on. Our house is built
not for haunting but for a love that shivers
with weeds and a mind of its own. You give

me the third word and it's a word that sounds
like history but feels like the Hollywood Hills
long before the world was born with a weapon
and dies in outer space.

FUN HOUSE II

It was freezing.
Something wanted to hurt us.
I could not speak. Nobody had returned.
What if I tell you that the face of a woman
is full of questions. The questions point away
from her body. The house conversed with mirrors.
The mirrors swallowed the screaming. The house
stopped breathing. The moon rose to the height
of its own occlusion. Hackles raised the memory
of red. You visualized the sound of breathing.
Because I dreamed, I was allowed my wounds.
Maybe we found a way to survive. With fishhooks.
Against instincts. Close your eyes. Break a window.
Anytime we were buried, dirt was nutritious.
Even the trees have learned to feed themselves.

I AM A PERSON OF HIDDEN TALENTS

Bloodshot and polarizing, I have yet to emit
gravitational pull or build a pill that will help
me come out of hiding. Realistic and complicated,
I was a ping-pong superstar before I got here. I can
shatter snow globes from across the room. Did you know
I am the god of transforming female pain into feathered
discs perfect for public consumption? People see me
as real, but not too real. My slight magnetism can
crack a crystal wristwatch when the tides go slack.
Heroic and hobbled, I know so much. Those swans
are beautiful. I am the problem that solves me.

WE WORK THE DARK LIKE THE MOON

Fur-bearing, itchy, and ruthlessly
consuming seasonal meats, we live
in a place where sunlight receives us
as a question. Hey, maybe we're just
another type of firmament pocked
with pulsing stars and the cotton lungs
of galaxies gone wild. At night, echoes
of Edelweiss make us crazy for schnitzel.
We string a little popcorn and light candles
for Jesus, the original comeback kid. Our skin
is brittle like a ship in a bottle. Everywhere
we look, winter is the body next to ours.
Decimated membranes and grain alcohol
take us from our families with a sigh
and we were never so close to sterilized.

A HUNDRED EFFORTS HAVE BEEN MADE

For the holiday party I make myself
a starfish costume of glitter and gray latex.
You say all the girls will be in the hospital
after this one, undone by chicken bones
or seizures. I say no, no one is trying that
hard to have fun. Dancing is difficult but
I perform mini-pinwheels with my body or
sometimes just my eyes, while the in-crowd
debates the ethics of space travel. Disguised
as a serial killer, you wear leather with bent
tendons and a winning smile. And we make
a charming couple and then we step into
a song by Elvis and go to hell all over again.
I drink and think: the older I get the fewer ways
there are to hurt myself and still learn something.
I find you in the kitchen, surrounded by olives
and tiny forks. Oh, I love forks and you, the joyful
conveyers of whatnot, needed. Something
I have touched and licked for years.

ON TRACK AT APPOMATTOX

Spring arrives like a bingo winner in a green church
basement so we go with a guidebook to Appomattox
on a bus. We tell the driver about our discomfort
in public toilets and where we got sick from the chicken.
Nice meadow. Rusted muskets, dusty winds and the sound
of sixty bags of chips ripped open. Look, it's a lodestone.
Look, it's a bone. Tumbling-mat antics of amorous rabbits.
Let's spread out, America. Our Kama Sutra couldn't
open a door. Catalpas pop. We resist the lure of time travel
and quasi-metaphysical chitchat. What if we killed Hitler?
What if Lincoln lived? Ask anyone thin-lipped at a window,
watching a flag come to the door. A battle always ends
with something permanently unhitched. Here's our own
Via Dolorosa, where the moon's a trap that won't give
us any more romance. The rabbi says, *Eat your bread in gladness*
but we feel so Roman today. We love. We hate.
We wait for the Clydesdales to bear us away.

COMPOS MENTIS

You remember how to pick a lock.
Forget the door. It is a representation
of metaphysical laziness. What excites
you is the tumblers' *chuck chuck chuck*.
When driven by an external source of
energy, the universe dissipates that energy
efficiently. No disrespect to the universe,
but there are too many rabbits. Too bad
you are the rabbit-keeper. Step aside,
there is a rabbit! He's fine right where he
is, but you? Your external source is not
energy. Your specific sadness is bringing
everyone down. Jupiter's huge gravity
helped save baby Earth. A rabbit running
in circles is actually thinking strategically.
Nothing is as random as they say it is.
You are born the weirdo that you are.

I AM FREE TO DESTROY MYSELF

And whosoever takes me, takes
me to Vegas to see the musical
of future humans versus ancient
gods. Pale Caesar's plutonium
glow makes me a fighter pilot
in a giant greenhouse where
artificial stars pop like blown
cartridges and I prepare for
cigarettes and mighty tipping.
Whosoever takes me to the hotel
where philosophy goes to remember
nothing plays it cool as I go to pieces
like a cheap mink in the swollen dunes
of red Naugahyde and chopsticks.
Tonight it's my right to order a $10
rib eye medium rare and go get lost
in America. My epiphanic hair goes
ballistic in the wind that geo-codes
a precise time of death into my DNA.
Now preverbal, now decompensating,
now split by a mescaline sense of grace,
I'm at the amphitheater with a cast of
thousands weeping at King Kong's steely
nemesis and love's abominable fist.

IN THE ABSENCE LIVES THE FEELING

Your love is not like washing a panda,
like a genial zookeeper, tireless promoter
of charismatic mammals. Nor is your
love a rubber bullet that really hurts but
won't leave a permanent mark. Also, your
love is not like the lies we tell about how
snakes can hypnotize their prey or how
everyone comes with a ghost built into her
space-age machine. I would not call your
love a trailer park, susceptible to jet streams
or fires ignited by an untended cigarette.
You never whip out your love like a camera
and snap a picture to treasure as our bodies
go to pieces. Certainly, your love is not an
allusion to French New Wave cinema—
it's not the first or last at the party. The type
of society your love is is not based on wage
labor. The names your love will not take:
Miss Congeniality. Tabitha. Goddess of Horses.

THE UNIVERSE CONTRACTING
AND EXPANDING

Winter diminishes me
so I sit in the house.
The house is anxious
so I give it a pill.
The pill is a helmet
so it is 100% safe.
Safe is a hotel where love
creeps, so romance abounds.
Romance is a microwave
so I am tender, then ruined.
Ruin is a family placid as furniture
so I transfigure its roots.
Roots thicken in winter so they
can carve names in the snow.
Snow is a broom so I sweep
the doom off all my beautiful.

Thanks to the editors of the publications where some of these poems first appeared, sometimes as earlier versions.

The Believer, Boston Review, Court Green, Indiana Review, La Petite Zine, Lush, Mudlark, Shade Poetry Annual.

Thanks to Melodee Monicken, Jan Pettit, Anne Piper, Kate Shuknecht, Jim Moore, Margaret Miles, Janet Bellingham, Lynn Bronson, Dale Gregory Anderson, Joni Tevis, and Tom and Judy Willoughby for their friendship, wisdom, reading, insight and love.

Hearty gratitude to Dana Levin and everyone at Milkweed Editions.

Jennifer Willoughby's poetry has appeared in the *Believer*, *Boston Review*, and the *Indiana Review*, among many others. She has received a McKnight Artist Fellowship, as well as the Academy of American Poets James Wright Award. A graduate of the University of Minnesota's MFA program, Willoughby works as a freelance advertising copywriter in the retail, tech, education, and healthcare industries. Born in Milwaukee, Wisconsin, Willoughby currently lives in Minneapolis, MN.

MILKWEED EDITIONS

and

THE LINDQUIST & VENNUM FOUNDATION

are pleased to announce the fourth award of

THE LINDQUIST & VENNUM PRIZE FOR POETRY

to

JENNIFER WILLOUGHBY

Established in 2011, the annual Lindquist & Vennum Prize for
Poetry awards $10,000 and publication by Milkweed Editions to
a poet residing in North Dakota, South Dakota, Minnesota, Iowa,
or Wisconsin. Finalists are selected from among all entrants by
the editors of Milkweed Editions. The winning collection is
selected annually by an independent judge. The 2015 Lindquist
& Vennum Prize for Poetry was judged by Dana Levin.

Milkweed Editions is one of the nation's leading independent
publishers, with a mission to identify, nurture and publish trans-
formative literature, and build an engaged community around
it. The Lindquist & Vennum Foundation was established by the
Minneapolis-headquartered law firm of Lindquist & Vennum,
LLP, and is a donor-advised fund of The Minneapolis Foundation.

Interior design by Mary Austin Speaker
Typeset in Apollo MT
by Mary Austin Speaker

Apollo was designed by Adrian Frutiger, a Swiss typographer, for the Monotype Corporation in 1964. Frutiger has designed over thirty typefaces, including Univers, Egyptienne, Linotype Didot and Avenir.